D0353004

LIST OF CO~~N~~

Preface

This collection of morning and evening prayers has grown primarily out of my own desire for a discipline and shape in daily personal prayer. During my time as Warden of Iona Abbey, Members and Associates of the Iona Community, whose first rule is to pray and study the Scriptures each day, often expressed the need for something like a prayer book for individual use. I hope these prayers may be helpful to them and to others as well.

Many people have indicated that they would like their own prayers at home to be based on the major themes of daily prayer at the Abbey, and so I have woven the weekly themes from Iona into this six-day cycle of prayer. On Mondays, there is an emphasis on justice and peace; on Tuesdays, a concentration on prayer for healing; on Wednesdays, a focus on the goodness of Creation and care for the earth, connected with the weekly pilgrimage around the island; on Thursdays, the theme of commitment to Christ; on Fridays, a celebration of the communion of the whole Church; and on Saturdays, an emphasis on welcome and hospitality. I have assumed that on Sundays the pattern is to gather together with others to pray rather than remaining alone.

I have included in the appendix a lectionary of psalms and gospel readings which have been used in the Abbey. This is based upon the 'Consultation on Common Texts' (1978), in which many churches participated, including the Roman Catholic, the Anglican, the Presbyterian and the Methodist.

Most of the prayers in this book, their rhythms and images, are drawn from and inspired by the work of Alexander Carmichael of Edinburgh. Late in the nineteenth century, Carmichael repeatedly visited the Scottish Hebrides to transcribe the prayers and poems of the people from the sung Gaelic, and eventually published them in the *Carmina Gadelica* in 1900 (recently republished by Floris Books, Edinburgh, 1992). These 'Songs and Prayers of the Gaels' had been forged by crofters and fishermen in the often wild and harsh conditions of the Western Isles, and been passed down in the oral tradition for hundreds of years. They were recited by both Roman Catholics and Protestants, for many of the prayers had their origins in the shared stream of spirituality that flowed from the Celtic Church of Ireland and Scotland before the eleventh century.

By the nineteenth century, however, as a result of the Highland Clearances and the dispersal of community, along with the suppression of Gaelic culture and language and ways of seeing, the songs were beginning to fade in the living memory. If Carmichael had not recorded these prayers, some of the greatest riches of Scottish spirituality would, within decades, have been lost forever. The *Carmina Gadelica* has played an important part on Iona and elsewhere in the upsurge of interest in our Celtic spiritual heritage.

Carmichael's prayers lend themselves to being used in the Iona Community's weekly cycle of themes. Christ is seen as being with and for the poor; healing is regarded as a grace that releases the essential life and health of body and soul, and not in opposition to the natural process of death; and the goodness of Creation is celebrated while life is also regarded as pilgrimage. Commitment to the gospel is set within the context of an intimate relationship with a personal God; the life of heaven and the life of earth are seen as bound inextricably together; and the delights and demands of welcome and hospitality - expecting to meet Christ in the stranger's guise - are richly portrayed.

The Iona Community thoughtfully provided me with a sabbatical and I used the time in part to work on this book of prayers. I trust that they will be of help to some of us, some of the time, in our prayers of wonder and hope for the world. They are offered in the conviction that our lives are enfolded by the great mystery of God, each day and each night.

TO MY MOTHER AND FATHER

WHO TAUGHT ME TO PRAY

THE LORD'S PRAYER

Our Father in heaven
Hallowed be your name
Your kingdom come
Your will be done
   on earth as in heaven
Give us today our daily bread
Forgive us our sins
As we forgive those who sin against us
Lead us not into temptation
But deliver us from evil
For the kingdom, the power
   and the glory are yours
Now and for ever
Amen.

Monday

JUSTICE AND PEACE

M O R N I N G

You have searched me
and known me O God
You know when I sit down
and when I rise up

(Ps 139. 1-2)

SILENCE

Be still
and aware of God's presence
within and all around

OPENING PRAYER
AND THANKSGIVING

Thanks be to you O God

that I have risen this day
To the rising of this life itself.
May it be a day of blessing,
O God of every gift,
A day of new beginnings given.
Help me to avoid every sin
And the source of every sin to forsake
And as the mist scatters
from the crest of the hills
May each ill haze clear
from my soul O God.

FREE PRAYERS OF THANKS

THE LORD'S PRAYER

SCRIPTURE READINGS

See appendix for psalms and gospels

SILENCE

Reflect on the gospel
and remember
that God is with those
who are poor and betrayed

INTERCESSIONS

O Christ of the poor and the yearning
Kindle in my heart within
A flame of love for my neighbour,
For my foe, for my friend,
    for my kindred all.
From the humblest thing that lives
To the Name that is highest of all
Kindle in my heart within
A flame of love.

Pray for the coming day
and for justice and peace

CLOSING PRAYER

This day and this night,
   may I know O God
The deep peace
   of the running wave
The deep peace
   of the flowing air
The deep peace
   of the quiet earth
The deep peace
   of the shining stars
The deep peace
   of the Son of Peace.

EVENING

You discern my thoughts
from far away O God
You search out my path
and my lying down
And are acquainted
with all my ways

(Ps 139. 2-3)

SILENCE
Be still
and aware of God's presence
within and all around

OPENING PRAYER
AND THANKSGIVING

O Christ of the least
    and the homeless
O Christ of the lost
    and betrayed
Come close to me this night
That I may come close to you.
As you watched me with care
    at my soul's shaping
Look on me now with grace.
As you blessed me with light
    at the sun's rising
Shine on me now with love.

FREE PRAYERS OF THANKS

THE LORD'S PRAYER

SCRIPTURE READINGS

SILENCE

Reflect on the gospel
and remember
that God is with those
who are poor and betrayed

INTERCESSIONS

Peace between nations
Peace between neighbours
Peace between lovers
In love of the God of life.
Peace between man and woman
Peace between parent and child
Peace between brother and sister
The peace of Christ above all peace.
Bless O Christ my face
Let my face bless everything.
Bless O Christ my eyes
Let my eyes bless all they see.

Recall the events of the day
and pray for justice and peace

CLOSING PRAYER

I end this day
as the Son of Mary would end it.
The grace of God be on this place
And on all whom
God has given me.
Who keeps watch
over us this night?
Who but the Christ of love.

Tuesday

PRAYERS FOR HEALING

MORNING

If I ascend to heaven
you are there O God
And if I make my bed in hell,
still you are with me

[Ps 139.8]

SILENCE

Be still
and aware of God's presence
within and all around

OPENING PRAYER AND THANKSGIVING

In the beginning O God
You shaped my soul and set its weave
You formed my body
      and gave it breath.
Renew me this day
      in the image of your love.
O great God, grant me your light
O great God, grant me your grace
O great God, grant me
      your joy this day
And let me be made pure
      in the well of your health.

FREE PRAYERS OF THANKS

THE LORD'S PRAYER

SCRIPTURE READINGS

SILENCE

Reflect on the gospel
and on the Christ of the cross,
suffering in the world
with all those who are broken

INTERCESSIONS

O Christ of the road
    of the wounded
O Christ of the tears
    of the broken
In me and with me
    the needs of the world
Grant me my prayers
    of loving and hoping
Grant me my prayers
    of yearning and healing.

Pray for the coming day
    and for healing
within and among people

CLOSING PRAYER

God before me, God behind me,
God above me, God beneath me.
I on your path O God
You, O God, on my way.
In the twistings of the road
In the currents of the river
Be with me by day
Be with me by night
Be with me by day and by night.

EVENING

You are behind me
and before me O God
You lay your hand
upon me

[Ps 139.5]

SILENCE

Be still
and aware of God's presence
within and all around

OPENING PRAYER
AND THANKSGIVING

As I utter these prayers
   from my mouth O God
In my soul may I feel your presence.
The knee that is stiff
   O healer make pliant
The heart that is hard,
 make warm beneath your wing
The wound that is giving me pain,
O best of healers, make whole
And may my hopes and my fears
Find a listening place with you.

FREE PRAYERS OF THANKS

THE LORD'S PRAYER

SCRIPTURE READINGS

SILENCE

Reflect on the gospel
and on the Christ of the cross,
suffering in the world
with all those who are broken

INTERCESSIONS

O God of the stars
    and the night skies
May your light be coming through
    thick clouds this night
On me and on everyone
    coming through dark tears
On each one in need
    and in suffering.

Recall the events of the day
    and pray for healing
within and among people

CLOSING PRAYER

Christ stands before me
    and peace is in his mind.
Sleep, O sleep
    in the calm of all calm
Sleep, O sleep
    in the love of all loves
Sleep I this night
    in the God of all life.

Wednesday

THE GOODNESS OF CREATION
AND CARE FOR THE EARTH

MORNING

It was you who formed
my inward parts.
You knit me together
in my mother's womb
I praise you
for I am fearfully
and wonderfully made

(Ps 139. 13–14)

SILENCE

Be still
and aware of God's presence
within and all around

OPENING PRAYER
AND THANKSGIVING

O Sun behind all suns

I give you greeting this new day.
Let all Creation praise you
Let the daylight
    and the shadows praise you
Let the fertile earth
    and the swelling sea praise you
Let the winds and the rain,
    the lightning and the thunder
    praise you
Let all that breathes,
    both male and female, praise you
And I shall praise you.
O God of all life
I give you greeting this day.

FREE PRAYERS OF THANKS

THE LORD'S PRAYER

SCRIPTURE READINGS

SILENCE

Reflect on the gospel
and on God
as the well-spring of all life

INTERCESSIONS

There is no plant in the ground
But tells of your beauty, O Christ.
There is no creature on the earth
There is no life in the sea
But proclaims your goodness.
There is no bird on the wing
There is no star in the sky
There is nothing beneath the sun
But is full of your blessing.
Lighten my understanding
of your presence all around, O Christ
Kindle my will
to be caring for Creation.

Pray for the coming day
and for the care of the earth

CLOSING PRAYER

Bless to me O God
My soul that comes from on high.
Bless to me O God
My body that is of earth.
Bless to me O God
Each thing my eye sees
Each sound my ear hears.
Bless to me O God
Each scent that goes to my nostrils
Each taste that goes to my lips
Each ray that guides my way.

EVENING

My frame
was not hidden from you
when I was being made
in secret
intricately woven
in the depths of the earth
Your eyes beheld
my unformed substance

(Ps 139.15)

SILENCE
Be still
and aware of God's presence
within and all around

OPENING PRAYER
AND THANKSGIVING

You are the love
   of each living creature O God
You are the warmth
   of the rising sun
You are the whiteness
   of the moon at night
You are the life
   of the growing earth
You are the strength
   of the waves of the sea.
Speak to me this night O God
Speak to me your truth.
Dwell with me this night O God
Dwell with me in love.

FREE PRAYERS OF THANKS

THE LORD'S PRAYER

SCRIPTURE READINGS

SILENCE

Reflect on the gospel
and on God
as the well-spring of all life

INTERCESSIONS

You are above me O God
You are beneath
You are in air
You are in earth
You are beside me
You are within.
O God of heaven,
you have made your home on earth
In the broken body of Creation.
Kindle within me
a love for you in all things.

Recall the events of the day
and pray for the care of the earth

CLOSING PRAYER

May the grace of the love
of the stars be mine
May the grace of the love
of the winds be mine
May the grace of the love
of the waters be mine
In the name of the Word
of all life.

Thursday

COMMITMENT TO CHRIST

MORNING

If I take the wings
of the morning
and settle at
the furthest limits of the sea
Even there your hand
shall lead me
and your right hand
shall hold me fast

(Ps 139. 9~10)

SILENCE
Be still
and aware of God's presence
within and all around

OPENING PRAYER
AND THANKSGIVING

O loving Christ
  who died upon the tree
Each day and each night
  I remember your love.
In my lying down
  and in my rising up
In life and in death
You are my health and my peace.
Each day and each night
  I remember your forgiveness
Bestowed on me so gently
  and generously
Each day and each night
  may I be fuller in love to you.

FREE PRAYERS OF THANKS

THE LORD'S PRAYER

SCRIPTURE READINGS

SILENCE

Reflect on the gospel
and on the One who calls us
to follow him
as the Way, the Truth and the Life

INTERCESSIONS

Life be in my speech
Truth in what I say.
The love Christ Jesus gave
Be filling every heart for me.
The love Christ Jesus gave
Be filling me for everyone.

Pray for the coming day
and to follow Christ more closely

CLOSING PRAYER

Bless to me O God
The earth beneath my feet.
Bless to me O God
The path on which I go.
Bless to me O God
The people whom I meet.
O God of all gods
bless to me my life.

If I say
"Surely the darkness
shall cover me
and the light around me
become night"
even the darkness
is not dark to you
The night is as bright
as the day, for darkness is
as light to you.

(Ps 139. 11–12)

SILENCE

Be still
and aware of God's presence
within and all around

OPENING PRAYER AND THANKSGIVING

I am bending my knee
In the eye of the God
   who created me
In the eye of the Son
   who died for me
In the eye of the Spirit
   who moves me
In love and in desire.
For the many gifts
   you have bestowed on me
Each day and night
   each sea and land
Each weather fair
   each calm each wild
Thanks be to you O God

FREE PRAYERS OF THANKS

THE LORD'S PRAYER

SCRIPTURE READINGS

SILENCE

Reflect on the gospel
and on the One who calls us
to follow him
as the Way, the Truth and the Life

INTERCESSIONS

O God I place myself
   with those who struggle
   this night.
I am here in need
I am here in pain
I am here alone
O God help me.

Recall the events of the day
and pray for those who suffer

CLOSING PRAYER

O Christ you are a bright flame
    before me
You are a guiding star above me
You are the light and love
    I see in others' eyes.
Keep me O Christ
    in a love that is tender
Keep me O Christ
    in a love that is true
Keep me O Christ
    in a love that is strong
Tonight, tomorrow and always.

Friday

THE COMMUNION OF
HEAVEN AND EARTH

MORNING

Where can I go
from your spirit O God?

(Ps 139.7)

SILENCE
Be still
and aware of God's presence
within and all around

OPENING PRAYER
AND THANKSGIVING

I awake this morning
In the presence
   of the holy angels of God.
May heaven open wide before me
Above me and around me
That I may see
   the Christ of my love
And his sunlit company
In all the things of earth this day.

FREE PRAYERS OF THANKS

THE LORD'S PRAYER

SCRIPTURE READINGS

SILENCE

Reflect on the gospel
and remember that we belong
to the whole company of saints
both past and present

INTERCESSIONS

O God of life, of all life, of each life,
I offer you my prayers
In the love of Christ
In the affection of Christ
In the company of Christ.
As your own household
    desires in heaven
So may I desire on earth this day.

Pray for the coming day
  and for the Church
  throughout the world

CLOSING PRAYER

The love and affection
   of the angels be with me
The love and affection
   of the saints be with me
The love and affection
   of heaven be with me
To lead me and to cherish me
   this day.

EVENING

Where can I flee
from your presence O God?

(Ps 139.7)

SILENCE

Be still
and aware of God's presence
within and all around

OPENING PRAYER
AND THANKSGIVING

My Christ, my love,
   my encircler,
Each day, each night,
Each light, each dark,
Be near me, uphold me,
My treasure, my truth.

FREE PRAYERS OF THANKS

THE LORD'S PRAYER

SCRIPTURE READINGS

SILENCE

Reflect on the gospel
and remember that we belong
to the whole company of saints
both past and present

INTERCESSIONS

Safeguard your faithful people
in the sanctuary of your love O God.
Shelter them this night
    in the shelter of the saints.
God to enfold them
God to surround them
God in their watching
God in their hoping
God in their sleeping
God in their ever-living souls.

Recall the events of the day
    and pray for the Church
throughout the world

CLOSING PRAYER

Grant to me, O Trinity of grace,
From whom all life freely flows
That no tie over-strict,
   no tie over-dear
May be between myself
   and this world.
As it was
As it is
As it shall be evermore,
With the ebb
With the flow
O Trinity of grace.

Saturday

WELCOME
AND HOSPITALITY

M O R N I N G

How weighty to me
are your thoughts O God
how vast is the sum of them
If I should count them
they are more than the sand
When I awake
I am still with you

(Ps 139.17-18)

SILENCE

Be still
and aware of God's presence
within and all around

OPENING PRAYER
AND THANKSGIVING

O God who brought me
    from the rest of last night
To the new light of this day
Bring me in the new light
    of this day
To the guiding light
    of the eternal.
Lead me O God
    on the journey of justice
Guide me O God
    on the pathways of peace
Renew me O God
    by the wellsprings of grace
Today, tonight and forever.

FREE PRAYERS OF THANKS

THE LORD'S PRAYER

SCRIPTURE READINGS

SILENCE

Reflect on the gospel
and remember
Jesus identifying himself
with the homeless
and the rejected

INTERCESSIONS

May those without shelter
    be under your guarding
    this day O Christ
May the wandering
    find places of welcome.
O son of the tears, of the wounds,
    of the piercings,
May your cross this day
    be shielding them.

Pray for the coming day
    and for refugees and those
without a place of welcome

CLOSING PRAYER

On my heart and on my house
The blessing of God.
In my coming and in my going
The peace of God.
In my life and in my seeking
The love of God.
At my end and new beginning
The arms of God to welcome me
and bring me home.

Search me O God
and know my heart
Test me and
know my thoughts
See if there is
any wicked way in me
and lead me
in the way everlasting

(Ps 139. 23~24)

SILENCE
Be still
and aware of God's presence
within and all around

OPENING PRAYER
AND THANKSGIVING

A shade are you in the heat O God
A shelter are you in the cold.
Eyes are you to the blind O God
A staff are you to the weak.
An island are you at sea O God
A rock are you on land.
O my soul's healer
Keep me at evening
Keep me at morning
Keep me at noon.
I am tired, astray and stumbling
Shield me from sin.
O my soul's healer
Shield me from sin.

FREE PRAYERS OF THANKS

THE LORD'S PRAYER

SCRIPTURE READINGS

SILENCE

Reflect on the gospel
and remember
Jesus identifying himself
with the homeless
and the rejected

INTERCESSIONS

Watch now O Christ
With those who are weary
    or wandering
    or weeping this night.
  Guide them to a house
    of your peace
And lead me to be caring
    for their tears.

Recall the events of the day
    and pray for refugees and those
without a place of welcome

CLOSING PRAYER

I lie down this night with God
And God will lie down with me.
I lie down this night with Christ
And Christ will lie down with me.
I lie down this night with the Spirit
And the Spirit will lie down with me.
The Three of my love
    will be lying down with me.
I shall not lie down with sin
Nor shall sin or sin's shadow
    lie down with me.
I lie down this night with God
And God will lie down with me.

A WEEKDAY LECTIONARY OF PSALMS AND GOSPEL READINGS

A lectionary is simply a list of Scripture readings. These are selected for use throughout the Church's year, which begins not on the 1 January but with Advent, four weeks before Christmas.

Christmastide is followed by the seasons of Epiphany and Lent. Ash Wednesday marks the beginning of Lent and is a preparation for the season of Easter. After the weeks of Easter, the long season of Pentecost begins and finally takes us back to Advent.

The key to using a lectionary is the calendar of movable feasts. Unlike Christmas, which always falls on the same date, other major feast days, such as Easter Sunday and Pentecost, change in date from year to year. This means that in following the lectionary, it is also necessary to keep an eye on the calendar of movable feasts. There are notes throughout the lectionary to indicate when the calendar of movable feasts should be checked as a guide.

CALENDAR OF MOVABLE FEASTS

YEAR	ASH WEDNESDAY	EASTER	ASCENSION	PENTECOST	FIRST SUNDAY OF ADVENT
1994	16 February	3 April	12 May	22 May	27 November
1995	1 March	16 April	25 May	4 June	3 December
1996	21 February	7 April	16 May	26 May	1 December
1997	12 February	30 March	8 May	18 May	30 November
1998	25 February	12 April	21 May	31 May	29 November
1999	17 February	4 April	13 May	23 May	28 November
2000	8 March	23 April	1 June	11 June	2 December
2001	28 February	15 April	24 May	3 June	3 December
2002	13 February	31 March	9 May	19 May	1 December
2003	5 March	20 April	29 May	8 June	30 November
2004	25 February	11 April	20 May	30 May	28 November

ADVENT

CHRISTMASTIDE

Advent 1
Week following Advent Sunday - see calendar of movable feasts.

Mon.	Ps. 51, Matt. 8.5-13
Tues.	Ps. 57, Luke 10.21-24
Wed.	Ps. 62, Matt. 15.29-39
Thurs.	Ps. 65, Matt. 7.21-27
Fri.	Ps. 67, Matt. 9.27-31
Sat.	Ps. 75, Matt. 9.35-38

Advent 2
Mon.	Ps. 77, Luke 5.17-26
Tues.	Ps. 80, Matt. 18.10-14
Wed.	Ps. 82, Matt. 11.25-30
Thurs.	Ps. 84, Matt. 11.11-15
Fri.	Ps. 85, Matt. 11.16-19
Sat.	Ps. 86, Matt. 17.10-13

Advent 3
Mon.	Ps. 90, Matt. 21.23-27
Tues.	Ps. 93, Matt. 21.28-32
Wed.	Ps. 95, Luke 7.18-23
Thurs.	Ps. 96, Luke 7.24-35
Fri.	Ps. 98, John 5.30-36
Sat.	Ps. 99, Matt. 1.1-17

Advent 4
If any of the days in Advent 4 fall on 24 December, go to the Christmastide readings in the next column.

Mon.	Ps. 100, Matt. 1.18-24
Tues.	Ps. 102, Luke 1.5-25
Wed.	Ps. 103, Luke 1.26-38
Thurs.	Ps. 104.1-34, Luke 1.39-45
Fri.	Ps. 107, Luke 1.46-56
Sat.	Ps. 111, Luke 1.57-66

Christmas Eve
24 Dec.   Ps. 113, Luke 1.67-79

Christmas Day
25 Dec.   Ps. 19, John 1.1-18

Feast of St Stephen
26 Dec.   Ps. 46, John 15.20-16.4

Feast of St John
27 Dec.   Ps. 103, John 13.21-35

Holy Innocents Day
28 Dec.   Ps. 128, Matt. 18.1-10

29 Dec.   Ps. 133 and 134, John 12.20-33

30 Dec.   Ps. 139.1-18, John 12.34-50

31 Dec.   Ps. 147, Luke 21.25-36

1 Jan.   Ps. 148, Luke 2.21-40

2 Jan.   Ps. 146, John 1.19-28

3 Jan.   Ps. 150, John 1.29-34

4 Jan.   Ps. 6, John 1.35-42

5 Jan.   Ps. 113, John 1.43-51

EPIPHANY

Days at the beginning of Epiphany
Feast of Epiphany falls on 6 Jan.
6 January   Ps. 8, Matt. 2.1-12
7 January   Ps. 96, John 2.1-12 *
8 January   Ps. 13, Matt. 6.24-34 *
9 January   Ps. 98, Mark 6.45-52 *
10 January Ps. 19, Luke 4.14-30 *
11 January Ps. 23, Luke 5.12-16 *
12 January Ps. 24, John 3.22-30 *

*If this day is a Monday go to the readings in the week Epiphany 1 below.

Epiphany 1
First full week after 6 January
Mon.   Ps. 27, Mark 1.14-20
Tues.   Ps. 30, Mark 1.21-28
Wed.   Ps. 33, Mark 1.29-39
Thurs. Ps. 46, Mark 1.40-45
Fri.   Ps. 29, Mark 2.1-12
Sat.   Ps. 85, Mark 2.13-17

Epiphany 2
Mon.   Ps. 121, Mark 2.18-22
Tues.   Ps. 42, Mark 2.23-28
Wed.   Ps. 126, Mark 3.1-6
Thurs. Ps. 50, Mark 3.7-12
Fri.   Ps. 51, Mark 3.13-19
Sat.   Ps. 67, Mark 3.20-30

Epiphany 3
Mon.   Ps. 57, Mark 3.31-35
Tues.   Ps. 62, Mark 4.1-9
Wed.   Ps. 65, Mark 4.10-20
Thurs. Ps. 85, Mark 4.21-25
Fri.   Ps. 86, Mark 4.26-34
Sat.   Ps. 96, Mark 4.35-41

Epiphany 4
Mon.   Ps. 77, Mark 5.1-20
Tues.   Ps. 99, Mark 5.21-43
Wed.   Ps. 80, Mark 6.1-6
Thurs. Ps. 82, Mark 6.7-13
Fri.   Ps. 84, Mark 6.14-29
Sat.   Ps. 100, Mark 6.30-44

Epiphany 5
Mon.   Ps. 90, Mark 6.53-56
Tues.   Ps. 93, Mark 7.1-13
Wed.   Ps. 95, Mark 7.14-23
Thurs. Ps. 98, Mark 7.24-30
Fri.   Ps. 102, Mark 7.31-37
Sat.   Ps. 103, Mark 8.1-10

Check the date of Ash Wednesday in the calendar of movable feasts, and then go to the appropriate week before Lent or to the Monday before Ash Wednesday.

Third week before Lent
Mon.   Ps. 127, Mark 8.11-13
Tues.   Ps. 128, Mark 8.14-21
Wed.   Ps. 107, Mark 8.22-26
Thurs. Ps. 126, Mark 8.27-33
Fri.   Ps. 111, Mark 8.34-38
Sat.   Ps. 114, Mark 9.1-13

Second week before Lent
Mon.   Ps. 6, Mark 9.14-29
Tues.   Ps. 8, Mark 9.30-37
Wed.   Ps. 133, Mark 9.38-41
Thurs. Ps. 13, Mark 9.42-50
Fri.   Ps. 75, Mark 10.1-12
Sat.   Ps. 113, Mark 10.13-16

First week before Lent
Mon.   Ps. 20, Mark 10.17-27
Tues.   Ps. 23, Mark 10.28-31
Wed.   Ps. 116, Mark 10.32-45
Thurs.   Ps. 118, Mark 10.46-52
Fri.   Ps. 139.1-18, Mark 11.11-26
Sat.   Ps. 24, Mark 11.27-33

LENT

Week in which Lent begins
Mon.   Ps. 57, Mark 12.1-12
Tues.   Ps. 103, Mark 12.13-17
Ash Wednesday
Wed.   Ps. 102, Matt. 6.1-21
Thurs.   Ps. 42, Luke 9.18-27
Fri.   Ps. 43, Matt. 9.14-17
Sat.   Ps. 46, Luke 5.27-32

Lent 1
Mon.   Ps. 51, Matt. 25.31-46
Tues.   Ps. 50, Luke 11.1-13
Wed.   Ps. 139.1-18, Luke 11.29-32
Thurs.   Ps. 62, Matt. 7.7-12
Fri.   Ps. 65, Matt. 5.21-26
Sat.   Ps. 67, Matt. 5.43-48

Lent 2
Mon.   Ps. 19, Luke 6.37-42
Tues.   Ps. 27, Matt. 23.1-12
Wed.   Ps. 75, Matt. 20.17-28
Thurs.   Ps. 77, Luke 16.19-31
Fri.   Ps. 30, Matt. 21.33-46
Sat.   Ps. 80, Luke 15.11-32

Lent 3
Mon.   Ps. 82, Luke 4.16-30
Tues.   Ps. 84, Matt. 18.21-35
Wed.   Ps. 86, Matt. 5.17-20

Thurs.   Ps. 90, Luke 11.14-23
Fri.   Ps. 93, Mark 12.28-34
Sat.   Ps. 95, Luke 18.9-14

Lent 4
Mon.   Ps. 99, John 4.43-54
Tues.   Ps. 103, John 5.1-18
Wed.   Ps. 104, John 5.19-29
Thurs.   Ps. 107, John 5.30-47
Fri.   Ps. 111, John 7.1-24
Sat.   Ps. 113, John 7.25-30

Lent 5
Mon.   Ps. 114, John 8.1-11
Tues.   Ps. 116, John 8.21-30
Wed.   Ps. 118, John 8.31-47
Thurs.   Ps. 121, John 8.48-59
Fri.   Ps. 123, John 10.22-42
Sat.   Ps. 43, John 11.45-57

Holy Week
Mon.   Ps. 25, John 12.1-11
Tues.   Ps. 27, John 12.37-50
Wed.   Ps. 22, John 13.21-35
Thurs.   Ps. 42, John 13.1-15
Fri.   Ps. 130, John 18.1-19.37
Sat.   Ps. 116, John 19.38-42

EASTER

Easter Week
Easter Day
Sun.   Ps. 113, John 20.1-18
Mon.   Ps. 122, Matt. 28.11-15
Tues.   Ps. 124, John 20.19-29
Wed.   Ps. 127, Luke 24.13-35
Thurs.   Ps. 133, 134, Luke 24.36-49
Fri.   Ps. 138, John 21.1-14
Sat.   Ps. 139.1-18, Mark 16.9-18

Easter 1

Mon.	Ps. 146, John 3.1-8
Tues.	Ps. 147, John 3.9-13
Wed.	Ps. 148, John 3.14-21
Thurs.	Ps. 150, John 3.31-36
Fri.	Ps. 46, John 6.1-15
Sat.	Ps. 29, John 6.16-21

Easter 2

Mon.	Ps. 8, John 6.22-29
Tues.	Ps. 13, John 6.30-35
Wed.	Ps. 16, John 6.35-40
Thurs.	Ps. 19, John 6.44-51
Fri.	Ps. 20, John 6.53-59
Sat.	Ps. 23, John 6.60-69

Easter 3

Mon.	Ps. 24, John 10.1-8
Tues.	Ps. 25, John 10.9-18
Wed.	Ps. 27, John 12.44-50
Thurs.	Ps. 29, John 13.16-20
Fri.	Ps. 30, John 14.1-6
Sat.	Ps. 33, John 14.7-14

Easter 4

Mon.	Ps. 42, John 14.21-26
Tues.	Ps. 43, John 14.27-31
Wed.	Ps. 46, John 15.1-8
Thurs.	Ps. 50, John 15.9-11
Fri.	Ps. 51, John 15.12-17
Sat.	Ps. 57, John 15.18-21

Easter 5

Mon.	Ps. 62, John 15.26-16.4
Tues.	Ps. 65, John 16.5-11
Wed.	Ps. 67, John 16.12-15
Ascension Day	
Thurs.	Ps. 96, Luke 24.44-53
Fri.	Ps. 75, John 16.20-23
Sat.	Ps. 77, John 16.24-28

Easter 6

Mon.	Ps. 121, John 16.29-33
Tues.	Ps. 126, John 17.1-11
Wed.	Ps. 138, John 17.12-19
Thurs.	Ps. 150, John 17.20-26
Fri.	Ps. 80, John 21.15-19
Sat.	Ps. 104.1-34, John 21.20-25

PENTECOST

The season of Pentecost can begin as early as 10 May and as late as 13 June. See the date of Pentecost in the calendar of movable feasts and go to the appropriate week.

Week beginning Sun. 8-14 May

Mon.	Ps. 82, Matt. 5.1-12
Tues.	Ps. 84, Matt. 5.13-16
Wed.	Ps. 85, Matt. 5.17-20
Thurs.	Ps. 86, Matt. 5.21-26
Fri.	Ps. 90, Matt. 5.27-32
Sat.	Ps. 93, Matt. 5.33-37

Week beginning 15-21 May

Mon.	Ps. 95, Matt. 5.38-42
Tues.	Ps. 96, Matt. 5.43-48
Wed.	Ps. 98, Matt. 6.1-6
Thurs.	Ps. 99, Matt. 6.7-15
Fri.	Ps. 100, Matt. 6.16-18
Sat.	Ps. 102, Matt. 6.19-23

Week beginning 22-28 May

Mon.	Ps. 103, Matt. 6.24-34
Tues.	Ps. 104.1-34, Matt. 7.1-6
Wed.	Ps. 107, Matt. 7.7-11
Thurs.	Ps. 111, Matt. 7.12-14
Fri.	Ps. 113, Matt. 7.15-20
Sat.	Ps. 114, Matt. 7.21-29

Week beginning 29 May - 4 June
Mon.   Ps. 116, Matt. 8.1-4
Tues.   Ps. 118, Matt. 8.5-13
Wed.   Ps. 121, Matt. 8.14-17
Thurs. Ps. 122, Matt. 8.18-22
Fri.   Ps. 123, Matt. 8.23-27
Sat.   Ps. 124, Matt. 8.28-34

Week beginning 5-11 June
Mon.   Ps. 126, Matt. 9.1-8
Tues.   Ps. 127, Matt. 9.9-13
Wed.   Ps. 128, Matt. 9.14-17
Thurs. Ps. 130, Matt. 9.18-26
Fri.   Ps. 133, 134, Matt. 9.27-31
Sat.   Ps. 138, Matt. 9.32-38

Week beginning 12-18 June
Mon.   Ps. 139.1-18, Matt. 10.1-7
Tues.   Ps. 146, Matt. 10.7-15
Wed.   Ps. 147, Matt. 10.16-23
Thurs. Ps. 148, Matt. 10.24-33
Fri.   Ps. 150, Matt. 10.34-39
Sat.   Ps. 6, Matt. 10.40-42

Week beginning 19-25 June
Mon.   Ps. 8, Matt. 11.1-6
Tues.   Ps. 13, Matt. 11.7-15
Wed.   Ps. 16, Matt. 11.16-19
Thurs. Ps. 19, Matt. 11.20-24
Fri.   Ps. 20, Matt. 11.25-27
Sat.   Ps. 22, Matt. 11.28-30

Week beginning 26 June - 2 July
Mon.   Ps. 23, Matt. 12.1-8
Tues.   Ps. 24, Matt. 12.14-21
Wed.   Ps. 25, Matt. 12.33-37
Thurs. Ps. 27, Matt. 12.38-42
Fri.   Ps. 29, Matt. 12.43-45
Sat.   Ps. 30, Matt. 12.46-50

Week beginning 3-9 July
Mon.   Ps. 33, Matt. 13.1-9
Tues.   Ps. 42, Matt. 13.10-17
Wed.   Ps. 43, Matt. 13.18-23
Thurs. Ps. 46, Matt. 13.24-30
Fri.   Ps. 50, Matt. 13.31-35
Sat.   Ps. 51, Matt. 13.36-43

Week beginning 10-16 July
Mon.   Ps. 57, Matt. 13.44-46
Tues.   Ps. 62, Matt. 13.47-52
Wed.   Ps. 65, Matt. 13.53-58
Thurs. Ps. 67, Matt. 14.1-12
Fri.   Ps. 75, Matt. 14.13-21
Sat.   Ps. 77, Matt. 14.22-36

Week beginning 17-23 July
Mon.   Ps. 80, Matt. 15.1-9
Tues.   Ps. 82, Matt. 15.10-20
Wed.   Ps. 84, Matt. 15.21-28
Thurs. Ps. 85, Matt. 15.29-31
Fri.   Ps. 86, Matt. 15.32-39
Sat.   Ps. 90, Matt. 16.1-4

Week beginning 24-30 July
Mon.   Ps. 93, Matt. 16.5-12
Tues.   Ps. 95, Matt. 16.13-23
Wed.   Ps. 96, Matt. 16.24-28
Thurs. Ps. 98, Matt. 17.1-8
Fri.   Ps. 99, Matt. 17.14-21
Sat.   Ps. 100, Matt. 17.22-27

Week beginning 31 July - 6 August
Mon.   Ps. 102, Matt. 18.1-14
Tues.   Ps. 103, Matt. 18.15-20
Wed.   Ps. 104.1-34, Matt. 18.21-35
Thurs. Ps. 107, Matt. 19.1-12
Fri.   Ps. 111, Matt. 19.13-15
Sat.   Ps. 113, Matt. 19.16-22

Week beginning 7-13 August
Mon.   Ps. 114, Matt. 19.23-30
Tues. Ps. 116, Matt. 20.1-16
Wed.   Ps. 118, Matt. 22.1-14
Thurs. Ps. 121, Matt. 22.34-40
Fri.   Ps. 122, Matt. 23.1-12
Sat.   Ps. 123, Matt. 23.13-22

Week beginning 14-20 August
Mon.   Ps. 124, Matt. 23.23-26
Tues. Ps. 126, Matt. 23.27-32
Wed.   Ps. 127, Matt. 24.42-51
Thurs. Ps. 128, Matt. 25.1-13
Fri.   Ps. 130, Matt. 25.14-30
Sat.   Ps. 133, 134, Matt. 25.31-40

Week beginning 21-27 August
Mon.   Ps. 138, Luke 4.16-30
Tues. Ps. 139.1-18, Luke 4.31-37
Wed.   Ps. 146, Luke 4.38-41
Thurs. Ps. 147, Luke 4.42-44
Fri.   Ps. 148, Luke 5.1-11
Sat.   Ps. 150, Luke 5.12-16

Week beginning 28 Aug. - 3 Sept.
Mon.   Ps. 6, Luke 5.17-26
Tues. Ps. 8, Luke 5.27-32
Wed.   Ps. 13, Luke 5.33-39
Thurs. Ps. 16, Luke 6.1-5
Fri.   Ps. 19, Luke 6.6-11
Sat.   Ps. 20, Luke 6.12-19

Week beginning 4-10 September
Mon.   Ps. 22, Luke 6.20-26
Tues. Ps. 23, Luke 6.27-31
Wed.   Ps. 24, Luke 6.32-36
Thurs. Ps. 25, Luke 6.37-38
Fri.   Ps. 27, Luke 6.39-42
Sat.   Ps. 29, Luke 6.43-49

Week beginning 11-17 September
Mon.   Ps. 30, Luke 7.1-10
Tues. Ps. 33, Luke 7.11-17
Wed.   Ps. 42, Luke 7.31-35
Thurs. Ps. 43, Luke 7.36-50
Fri.   Ps. 46, Luke 8.1-3
Sat.   Ps. 50, Luke 8.4-15

Week beginning 18-24 September
Mon.   Ps. 51, Luke 8.16-18
Tues. Ps. 57, Luke 8.19-21
Wed.   Ps. 62, Luke 9.1-6
Thurs. Ps. 65, Luke 9.7-9
Fri.   Ps. 67, Luke 9.18-22
Sat.   Ps. 75, Luke 9.44-45

Week beginning 25 Sept. - 1 Oct.
Mon.   Ps. 80, Luke 9.46-50
Tues. Ps. 82, Luke 9.51-56
Wed.   Ps. 84, Luke 9.57-62
Thurs. Ps. 85, Luke 10.1-12
Fri.   Ps. 86, Luke 10.13-16
Sat.   Ps. 90, Luke 10.17-24

Week beginning 2-8 October
Mon.   Ps. 93, Luke 10.25-37
Tues. Ps. 95, Luke 10.38-42
Wed.   Ps. 96, Luke 11.1-4
Thurs. Ps. 98, Luke 11.5-13
Fri.   Ps. 99, Luke 11.14-26
Sat.   Ps. 100, Luke 11.27-28

Week beginning 9-15 October
Mon.   Ps. 102, Luke 11.29-32
Tues. Ps. 103, Luke 11.37-41
Wed.   Ps. 104.1-34, Luke 11.42-46
Thurs. Ps. 107, Luke 11.47-54
Fri.   Ps. 111, Luke 12.1-7
Sat.   Ps. 113, Luke 12.8-12

Week beginning 16-22 October
Mon.   Ps. 114, Luke 12.13-21
Tues.   Ps. 116, Luke 12.35-40
Wed.   Ps. 118, Luke 12.41-48
Thurs. Ps. 121, Luke 12.49-53
Fri.   Ps. 122, Luke 12.54-59
Sat.   Ps. 123, Luke 13.1-9

Week beginning 23-29 October
Mon.   Ps. 124, Luke 13.10-17
Tues.   Ps. 126, Luke 13.18-21
Wed.   Ps. 127, Luke 13.22-30
Thurs. Ps. 128, Luke 13.31-35
Fri.   Ps. 130, Luke 14.1-6
Sat.   Ps. 133, 134, Luke 14.7-11

Week beginning 30 Oct. - 5 Nov.
Mon.   Ps. 138, Luke 14.12-14
Tues.   Ps. 139.1-18, Luke 14.15-24
Wed.   Ps. 146, Luke 14.25-33
Thurs. Ps. 147, Luke 15.1-10
Fri.   Ps. 148, Luke 16.1-8
Sat.   Ps. 150, Luke 16.9-15

Week beginning 6-12 November
Mon.   Ps. 6, Luke 17.1-6
Tues.   Ps. 8, Luke 17.7-10
Wed.   Ps. 13, Luke 17.11-19
Thurs. Ps. 16, Luke 17.20-25
Fri.   Ps. 19, Luke 17.26-37
Sat.   Ps. 20, Luke 18.1-8

Week beginning 13-19 November
Mon.   Ps. 22, Luke 18.35-43
Tues.   Ps. 23, Luke 19.1-10
Wed.   Ps. 24, Luke 19.11-28
Thurs. Ps. 25, Luke 19.41-44
Fri.   Ps. 27, Luke 19.45-48
Sat.   Ps. 29, Luke 20.27-40

Week Before Advent
Mon.   Ps. 30, Luke 21.1-4
Tues.   Ps. 33, Luke 21.5-11
Wed.   Ps. 42, Luke 21.12-19
Thurs. Ps. 43, Luke 21.20-28
Fri.   Ps. 46, Luke 21.29-33
Sat.   Ps. 50, Luke 21.34-38

THE IONA COMMUNITY

The Iona Community owes its very existence to the continuing conviction that Christian community is not an abstract utopian vision, but is to be discovered, pursued and celebrated at street level and in the very midst of life.

The roots of the Iona Community extend back to 1938, to the late George MacLeod's vision to rebuild the medieval abbey which lay on the site of Saint Columba's sixth-century monastic settlement on Iona, on the West Coast of Scotland. Iona was renowned as an important centre of Celtic Christianity and the Benedictines began building the Abbey in the thirteenth century. It flourished and grew until the Reformation when it fell into disrepair. In 1938, George MacLeod, who as a minister in industrial Glasgow had felt most keenly the huge gulf between the Church and the working people of that time, led skilled craftsmen and ministers to work together to rebuild the abbey and forge the beginnings of a Christian community based on the idea that faith finds reality in the workings of everyday life.

Today, the Iona Community is an ecumenical organisation. It is part of the Church of Scotland but it is open to people of any denomination. Members are men and women, lay and ordained, from Scotland, England and other parts of the world, whose commitment to the Community is expressed in their ordinary places of life and work, in prayer, economic sharing, meeting together and working towards justice and peace. More than a thousand Associates support the Community's work through daily prayer and financial contribution, while Friends of the Community also offer financial support.

At the Abbey and the MacLeod Centre on Iona, and at Camas on Mull, a small resident group of staff and volunteers welcome guests to share in a common life of work, worship and recreation. The Community's leader, administrative staff, Wild Goose Resource Group, youth development worker and publishing section are based in Govan, Glasgow, where George MacLeod originally had his ministry, while it also funds a peace worker based in Perthshire. Through all these different strands the vision of Christian community develops and evolves and, as one of the community's prayers puts it, new ways are sought 'to touch the hearts of all'.

For more information contact
The Iona Community, Pearce Institute, Govan, Glasgow G51 3UU
Phone 041 445 4561 Fax. 041 445 4295

OTHER TITLES FROM WILD GOOSE PUBLICATIONS

SONGBOOKS with full music
(titles marked * have companion cassettes)
... PSALMS OF PATIENCE, PROTEST AND PRAISE* John Bell
... HEAVEN SHALL NOT WAIT (Wild Goose Songs Vol.1)* John Bell and Graham Maule
... ENEMY OF APATHY (Wild Goose Songs Vol.2) John Bell and Graham Maule
... LOVE FROM BELOW (Wild Goose Songs Vol.3)* John Bell and Graham Maule
... INNKEEPERS & LIGHT SLEEPERS* (for Christmas) JohnBell
... MANY & GREAT (Songs of the World Church Vol.1)* John Bell (ed./arr.)
... SENT BY THE LORD (Songs of the World Church Vol.2)* John Bell (ed./arr.)
... FREEDOM IS COMING* Anders Nyberg (ed.)
... PRAISING A MYSTERY, Brian Wren
... BRING MANY NAMES, Brian Wren

CASSETTES & CDs
(titles marked † have companion songbooks)
... CD, PSALMS OF PATIENCE, PROTEST AND PRAISE, Wild Goose Worship Group
... Tape, PSALMS OF PATIENCE, PROTEST AND PRAISE, Wild Goose Worship Group
... Tape, HEAVEN SHALL NOT WAIT† Wild Goose Worship Group
... Tape, LOVE FROM BELOW† Wild Goose Worship Group
... Tape, INNKEEPERS & LIGHT SLEEPERS† (for Christmas) Wild Goose Worship Group
... Tape, MANY & GREAT† Wild Goose Worship Group
... Tape, SENT BY THE LORD† Wild Goose Worship Group
... Tape, FREEDOM IS COMING† Fjedur
... Tape, TOUCHING PLACE, A, Wild Goose Worship Group
... Tape, CLOTH FOR THE CRADLE, Wild Goose Worship Group

DRAMA BOOKS
... EH JESUS...YES PETER No. 1, John Bell and Graham Maule
... EH JESUS...YES PETER No. 2, John Bell and Graham Maule
... EH JESUS...YES PETER No. 3, John Bell and Graham Maule
... WILD GOOSE PRINTS No. 1, John Bell and Graham Maule
... WILD GOOSE PRINTS No. 2, John Bell and Graham Maule
... WILD GOOSE PRINTS No. 3, John Bell and Graham Maule
... WILD GOOSE PRINTS No. 4 (On the way to the cross), John Bell and Graham Maule
... WILD GOOSE PRINTS No. 5, John Bell and Graham Maule
... WILD GOOSE PRINTS No. 6 (Christmas scripts) John Bell and Graham Maule

PRAYER/LITURGICAL BOOKS
... IONA COMMUNITY WORSHIP BOOK, THE
... WEE WORSHIP BOOK, A, Wild Goose Worship Group
... WHOLE EARTH SHALL CRY GLORY, THE, George MacLeod

OTHER BOOKS
... FALLEN TO MEDIOCRITY: CALLED TO EXCELLENCE, Erik Cramb
... RE-INVENTING THEOLOGY AS THE PEOPLE'S WORK, Ian Fraser
... WAY TO GOD, A – A BIOGRAPHY OF GEORGE MORE, Mary More